VERÖFFENTLICHUNGEN MITTELALTERLICHER MUSIKHANDSCHRIFTEN

NR. 6

PUBLICATIONS OF MEDIAEVAL MUSICAL MANUSCRIPTS

NO. 6

OXFORD, LATIN LITURGICAL D 20
LONDON, ADD. MS. 25031
CHICAGO, MS. 654APP.

Faksimile, Einleitung
Register und Transcriptionen

Facsimile, Introduction
Index and Transcriptions

Von

By

LUTHER DITTMER

Institute of Mediaeval Music
1751 West 9th Street
Brooklyn 23, N.Y.
U.S.A.

Eine Auflage von	An Edition of
600 Exemplaren	600 Copies

№ 328

LATIN LITURGICAL D 20

Mit diesem Band wird die Veröffentlichungen der bisher bekannten Worcester Fragmente vervollständigt. Diese Bruchstücke, die die wichtigste praktische Quelle zur Erforschung der englischen mehrstimmigen Musik gemeinsamer Provenienz aus dem 13. und beginnenden 14. Jahrhundert bieten, werden heute in drei Bibliotheken aufbewahrt. Einige Fragmente findet man *in situ* in der Kapitelsbibliothek in Worcester unter Signatur *Add. 68*; Photokopien dieser Sammlung wurden weitgehend im fünften Band dieser Veröffentlichungsreihe (*Worcester Add. 68, Westminster Abbey 33327* und *Madrid Bibl. nac. 192*) veröffentlicht und besprochen. Andere Bruchstücke befinden sich zur Zeit im British Museum in London unter Signatur *Add. 25031* und in der Bodleian Library in Oxford in der Handschrift neuer Zusammensetzung *latin liturgical d 20*; diese Sammlungen werden hier hauptsächlich behandelt.

Die Handschrift *lat. lit. d 20* besteht heute aus 40 folios, die als 1-27, 27a, 28-33, 34^{v} (die *verso* Seite ist als eine *recto* gebunden) und 35-39 bezeichnet sind, wovon die aus den Oxforder Handschriften *Auct. F inf. 1,3, Bodley 862* und *Hatton 30* entnommenen Blätter Originale sind; die übrigen aus Worcester *Add. 68 Fragmente IX, X, XIII, XXVIII, XXXI* und *XXXV* (ehemals Oxford, *Magdallen College 100*) sowie British Museum *Add. 25031* sind Photokopien. F. 27a besteht aus umgekehrten Photokopien des mit Leim verfestigten Abdruckes der

LATIN LITURGICAL D 20

The publication of all of the Worcester Fragments discovered to date is completed with this volume. These fragments, which form the most important practical source of common provenience for research into English polyphonic music of the 13th and the beginning of the 14th centuries, are now preserved in three libraries. Certain leaves are preserved *in situ* in the Chapter Library in Worcester under call number *Add. 68*; photographs of this collection were published and discussed for the most part in the fifth volume of this series (*Worcester Add. 68, Westminster Abbey 33327* and *Madrid Bibl. nac. 192*). Other fragments may be found in the British Museum in London under call number *Add. 25031* and in the Bodleian Library in Oxford in a recently established manuscript *latin liturgical d 20*; these collections will be chiefly presented in this volume.

The manuscript *lat. lit. d 20* now consists of 40 folios, which are designated as 1-27, 27a, 28-33, 34^{v} (the verso side is bound as a recto) and 35-39, whereby those leaves which have been removed from the Oxford manuscripts *Auct. F inf. 1,3, Bodley 862* and *Hatton 30* are originals; the remainder from Worcester *Add. 68 Fragments IX, X, XIII, XXVIII, XXXI* and *XXXV* (formerly Oxford, *Magdallen College 100*) as well as British Museum *Add. 25031* consists of photographic reproductions. F. 27a consists of reversed photocopies of the impression fastened

vorderen und hinteren Innenseiten des Deckels; dabei ist f. 27a^r = f. 28^r, während das zu f. 27a^v passende Blatt fehlt. In dieser Ausgabe wird stets auf die Signatur des einzelnen Fragments hingewiesen, während die Foliozahl der Photokopien in *lat. lit. d 20* in Klammern aufgeführt wird.

Es liegt in der Art der Veröffentlichung dieser Bruchstücke, dass sie in verschiedenen Büchern abgedruckt und besprochen werden. Das vorliegende Heft beschäftigt sich mit dem Problem der Zusammensetzung der gedruckten Ausgaben, die wesentlich die in der Handschrift *lat. lit. d 20* enthaltenen Kompositionen behandeln. Faksimiles sämtlicher in *lat. lit. d 20* enthaltenen Blätter, sowie Photokopien sind in folgenden Veröffentlichungen abgedruckt:

by glue to the front and rear inner sides of the cover; thereby f. 27a^r = f. 28^r, whereas the leaf which would have fitted to f. 27a^v is missing. In this edition, the call number of the original leaf is given, whereas the number of the folio of the photograph in *lat. lit. d 20* is given in parentheses.

The manner in which these fragments have been published accounts for the fact that they are printed and discussed in many different books. The present volume concerns itself chiefly with a compilation of the printed editions, which concern themselves with the compositions preserved in *lat. lit. d 20*. Facsimiles of all of the leaves preserved in *lat. lit. d 20* as well as of the photographs are printed in the following publications:

Bs Manfred Bukofzer, *Sumer is icumen in, A Revision,* in University of California publications in Music, 1944.

Dd Luther Dittmer, *Auszug aus The Worcester Music Fragments,* Institute of Mediaeval Music, 1957.

DO Luther Dittmer, *Oxford, Bodleian Library, latin liturgical d 20, University of Chicago, 654 app.,* Institute of Mediaeval Music, 1959.

DW Luther Dittmer, *Worcester Add. 68, Westminster Abbey 33327, Madrid, Bibl. nac. 192,* Institute of Mediaeval Music, 1958.

EEH *Early English Harmony,* Vol. I, ed. H. E. Wooldridge, 1897.

F & H J. K. Floyer & S. G. Hamilton, *Catalogue of Manuscripts preserved in the Chapter Library of Worcester Cathedral,* 1906.

WF Luther Dittmer, *The Worcester Fragments,* American Institute of Musicology, 1957.

WMH Dom Anselm Hughes, *Worcester Mediaeval Harmony,* the Plainsong and Mediaeval Music Society, 1928.

Die Faksimiles der in *lat. lit. d 20* enthaltenen Blätter (* bezeichnet eine Photokopie) sind folgendermassen verteilt:

Facsimiles of the leaves contained in *lat. lit. d 20* (* designates a photographic reproduction) are distributed as follows:

Folio

		14^r	23 N	*27^v	*DW* 22-23
*1^r	*DW* 24	14^v	24 O	*27a^r	40 DD
*1^v	*Dd* 28	15^r	25 P	*27a^v	39 EE
*2^r	*Dd* 29	15^v	26 Q	28^r	41 FF
*2^v	*Dd* 30	16^r	27 R	28^v	42 GG
*3^r	11 A	16^v	*WMH* 32	*29^r	*DW* 67
*3^v	12 B	17^r	28 S	*29^v	*WF* 66
*4^r	*WMH* 127	17^v	*WMH* 139	*30^r	*WF* 67
*4^v	13 C	18^r	*WMH* 139	*30^v	*DW* 65
*5^r	14 D	18^v	29 T	*31^r	*DW* 69
*5^v	15 E	19^r	30 U	*31^v	*EEH* pl. 40
*6^r	16 F	19^v	31 V	*32^r	*DW* 68
*6^v	17 G	*20^r	*DW* 25	*32^v	*WMH* 55
*7^r	*WMH* 63	*20^v	*DW* 26	*33^r	*WMH* frontispiece
*7^v	*WF* 62	*21^r	32 W	*33^v	*DW* 66
*8^r	*WF* 63	*21^v	33 X	34^r	43 JJ
*8^v	18 H	22^r	*Bs* 90	34^v	43 KK
*9^r	*Dd* 21	22^v	*Bs* 92	35^r	44 LL
*9^v	*WMH* 128	23^r	34 Y	35^v	45 MM
*10^r	*WMH* 129	23^v	35 Z	*36^r	*DW* 28
*10^v	*DW* 48	24^r	36 AA	*36^v	Dd 22
*11^r	*DW* 49	24^v	37 BB	*37^r	*Dd* 23
*11^v	*DW* 50	25^r	38 CC	*37^v	*DW* 29
12^r	19 J	25^v	*WF* 64	*38^r	*DW* 30
12^v	20 K	*26^r	*WF* 65	*38^v	*Dd* 24
13^r	21 L	*26^v	*DW* 70	*39^r	*Dd* 25
13^v	22 M	*27^r	*DW* 20-21	*39^v	*DW* 31

Buchstaben, nach der auf diesen Band bezogenen Seitenzahl, gehen auf die Bezeichnungen in den in *DW* S. 7-13 vorzufindenen Registern zurück. Als Ergänzung zu den Verzeichnissen *DW* S. 7-8 (Register der Faksimiles der Fragmente in Worcester *Add. 68*), *DW* S. 8-9 (Register der Faksimiles der Blätter und Photokopien in *lat. lit. d 20*) und *DW* S. 9-13 (vollständiges Verzeichnis der Textanfänge der Worcester Kompositionen sowie ihrer Faksimilierung) werden

Letters after those page numbers which designate facsimiles in this volume refer to the appropriate ciphers in the indices in *DW* p. 7-13. As an addition to the lists *DW* p. 7-8 (index of the facsimiles of the fragments in Worcester *Add. 68*), *DW* p. 8-9 (index of the facsimiles of the leaves and photographic reproductions in *lat. lit. d 20*) and *DW* p. 9-13 (complete index of the textual incipits of the Worcester compositions as well as their

Worcester *Add. 68 Frag. XI* ff. 2^r und 2^v auf Seiten 32 und 33 (W und X), *Frag. XXVIII* f. $a1^v$ auf Seite 42 (GG) und *Frag. XXXII* recto und verso auf Seiten 46 und 47 (NN und OO) hier faksimiliert. Es erübrigt sich ein wiederholtes Verzeichnis der Textanfänge neben dem Ort der Veröffentlichung zu geben.

Sämtliche lesbare mehrstimmige Kompositionen der Worcester Fragmente sind in *WF* in Übertragung geboten, wobei die Nummerierung der einzelnen Kompositionen der Reihe der Fragmente in *lat. lit. d 20* (Nr. 1-77) sowie der nicht in *lat. lit. d 20* vertretenen Fragmente aus Worcester *Add. 68* (78-109) folgt; Zusatzbuchstaben bezeichnen die nicht übertragenen Kompositionen. *WF* bietet ausserdem S. 14-15 ein Verzeichnis der Grössen der einzelnen Fragmente, der ursprünglichen Zusammengehörigkeit der Blätter und allfällige alte Foliozahlen für *lat. lit. d 20*; S. 48-49 ein gleiches für Worcester *Add. 68*; S. 18-28 eine Liste der Kompositionen mit Angaben über Foliozahl und Systeme der einzelnen Stimmen für *lat. lit. d 20*; S. 50-55 ein gleiches für Worcester *Add. 68*; S. 28-30 ein Verzeichnis der Musikgattungen der einzelnen Kompositionen nebst der Tenorquelle für *lat. lit. d 20*; S. 55-56 ein gleiches für Worcester *Add. 68*; S. 30-32 Konkordanzen der in *lat. lit. d 20* sich befindenden Kompositionen; S. 56-57 ein gleiches für die in Worcester *Add. 68*; S. 33-35 Stimmtausch in den einzelnen Kompositionen in *lat. lit. d 20*; S. 57-58 ein gleiches für die in

availability in facsimiles), the following facsimiles are included here: Worcester *Add. 68 Frag. XI* ff. 2^r and 2^v on pages 32 and 33 (W and X), *Frag. XXVIII* f. $a1^v$ on page 42 (GG) and *Frag. XXXII* recto and verso on pages 46 and 47 (NN and OO). It is thus unnecessary to repeat an index of textual incipits combined with their place of publication.

All of the legible polyphonic compositions of the Worcester Fragments are offered in transcription in *WF*, whereby the numbering of the individual compositions follows the sequence of the leaves in *lat. lit. d 20* (Nos. 1-77) as well as of those fragments from Worcester *Add. 68* which are not contained in *lat. lit. d 20* (Nos. 78-109); the addition of a letter to a number indicates a composition not transcribed. In addition, *WF* offers on p. 14-15 an index of the dimensions of the individual leaves, information concerning the original grouping of the leaves as well as any older foliation of the leaves for *lat. lit. d 20*; p. 50-55 similarly for Worcester *Add. 68*; p. 28-30 an index of the musical genera of the individual compositions as well as the sources of the tenor for *lat. lit. d 20*; p. 55-56 similarly for Worcester *Add. 68*; p. 30-32 concordances for the compositions found in *lat. lit. d 20*; p. 56-57 similarly for those in Worcester *Add. 68*; p. 33-35 *Stimmtausch* (interchange of melodic material among the voices) in the individual compositions in *lat. lit. d 20*; p. 57-58 similarly for those in Worcester *Add. 68*. Information about the sources for

Worcester *Add. 68*. Notizen über die Quellen befinden sich für *lat. lit. d 20* auf S. 15-17; für Worcester *Add. 68* auf S. 49-50; Notizen über die einzelnen Kompositionen befinden sich für die in *lat. lit. d 20* vorzufindenden Kompositionen auf S. 35-48; für die in *Add. 68* auf S. 58-61.

lat. lit. d 20 may be found on p. 15-17, for Worcester *Add. 68* on p. 49-50. Information about the individual compositions in *lat. lit. d 20* may be found on p. 35-48, for *Add. 68* on p. 58-61.

Dd S. 16-20 enthält ein Verzeichnis der Textanfänge der einzelnen Kompositionen, wobei auf die Seite der Besprechung in folgenden Aufsätzen hingewiesen wird:

Dd p. 16-20 contains an index of textual incipits of the individual compositions, whereby each entry gives a cross-reference to the page of the discussion in the following essays:

Binary Rhythm, Musical Theory and the Worcester Fragments, in **Musica Disciplina**, VII 1953, S. 27-57.

An English Discantuum Volumen, in **Musica Disciplina**, VIII 1954, S. 19-58.

Endlich darf auf zwei weitere Veröffentlichungen verwiesen werden, die einzelne Kompositionen besprechen. Ein Verzeichnis der in diesen Aufsätzen angeführten Kompositionen folgt:

Finally, one may make reference to two further publications, which discuss individual compositions. An index of the compositions included in these essays follows:

The Dating and the Notation of the Worcester Fragments, in **Musica Disciplina**, XI 1957, S. 5-11.

Beiträge zum Studium der Worcester Fragmente, in **Die Musikforschung**, X 1957, S. 29-39.

Worcester Nr.	
5	*Beiträge* 32
9	*Beiträge* 33-34
25	*Beiträge* 31
31	*Beiträge* 32
41	*Dating* 6
43	*Dating* 6
44	*Dating* 6
45	*Beiträge* 39

Worcester No.	
47	*Dating* 6
48	*Dating* 6
53	*Dating* 7
67	*Dating* 6-8
69	*Beiträge* 31
80	*Beiträge* 34
81	*Dating* 8
94	*Beiträge* 31
95	*Beiträge* 39

CHICAGO, Hs. 654 app.

Die vorderen und hinteren Vorsatzblätter der aus der Abtei Meaux stammenden Sammelhandschrift des 13. und 14. Jahrhunderts, Chicago Hs. *654*, die jetzt aus dem Kodex losgelöst und als *654 app.* aufbewahrt werden, enthalten mehrstimmige geistliche Gesänge, die eng mit der Musik des Worcester Kreises verbunden sind. Sie wurden von dem Anglisten Richard L. Greene entdeckt, der sie vorläufig besprochen hat [1].

Es handelt sich um vier Blätter, eventuell zwei Doppelblätter eines Kodex, die die Mitte einer Lage hätten bilden können. Da die ursprüngliche Grösse dieser Fragmente (etwa 28 x 20 cm.) etwa doppelt so gross wie der Band (13 x 10 cm.) war, wurde jedes Bruchstück aufgeschnitten, sodass in jedem Falle die Mitte des Blattes fehlt. Wie im Falle der Musik der Worcester Fragmente und anderer mehrstimmiger Musik in den Britischen Inseln des 13. und angehenden 14. Jahrhunderts, veraltete der Stil dieser Kompositionen rasch gegen Ende des 14. Jahrhunderts, und eine neue Welle des musikalischen Schaffens während der Epoche von Dunstable trat an ihre Stelle. Deswegen erfolgte die Aufteilung der Hand-

---

1) R. L. Greene, *Two Medieval Musical Manuscripts: Egerton 3307 and Some University of Chicago Fragments*, in the *Journal of the American Musicological Society*, VII 1954, S. 1-34.

CHICAGO, Ms. 654 app.

The front and rear flyleaves of the 13th and 14th century composite manuscript from Meaux Abbey, Chicago Ms. *654*, which have now been removed from their codex and are preserved as *654 app.*, contain polyphonic religious compositions, which are closely connected with the music of the Worcester school. They were discovered by the anglicist Richard L. Greene, who has presented us with an interim report [1]:

These fragments consist of four leaves, perhaps even two bifolios, which may have formed the middle of a gathering. Since the original dimensions of these fragments (approximately 28 x 20 cm.) were approximately twice the size of the codex (13 x 10 cm.), every fragment was cut in half, so that the middle of every leaf is missing. Just as in the case of the music of the Worcester Fragments and of other polyphonic music of the 13th and beginning 14th centuries in the British Isles, the musical style of these compositions quickly suffered obsolescence toward the end of the 14th century, and a new wave of musical creativity occupied their place during the epoch of Dunstable. Consequently, the

---

1) R. L. Greene, *Two Medieval Musical Manuscripts: Egerton 3307 and Some University of Chicago Fragments*, in the *Journal of the American Musicological Society*, VII 1954, p. 1-34.

schrift wohl in der ersten Hälfte des 15. Jahrhunderts. Schon R. Greene (S. 29) hat gezeigt, dass diese Vorsatzblätter vor 1452 zum Kodex gehört haben müssen, da der Name Walter*us* Giffard auf eine der Notenfragmente als Ergänzung zu der gegenüberliegenden vor 1452 zusammengestellten Liste der Erzbischöfe zu York im Hauptkodex geschrieben wurde. Ausser der Tatsache aber, dass diese Fragmente schon innerhalb etwa hundert Jahre nach ihrer Entstehung in Meaux vorzufinden waren, ist kein zwingender Grund vorhanden, sie mit dieser Pflegestätte zu verbinden. Immerhin wollen wir sie vorläufig für diese Provenienz halten.

Da nur die dritte Komposition *In excelsis gloria* [1] in der vorliegenden Form bisher in anderen Quellen bekannt ist, werden alle die anderen Gesänge in Übertragung geboten, in wie weit sie rekonstruiert werden konnten. Die in Klammern stehenden Ziffern beziehen sich auf die Ludwig'schen Motettennummern. Der Inhalt schliesst der Reihe nach ein:

partition of the codex occured undoubtedly in the first half of the 15th century. R. Greene has already shown (p. 29), that these flyleaves must already have belonged to the main codex before 1452, since the name Walter*us* Giffard has been written onto one of the musical fragments as an addition to the list of archbishops in York *en face* in the main codex. With the exception of the fact, that these fragments were to be found in Meaux about a hundred years after their origin, there is no compelling reason to connect them with that center. For the time being, however, we wish to consider them to be of this provenience.

Since only the third composition *In excelsis gloria* [1] has been identified in its present form in other sources, all of the other compositions are offered in transcription, to the extent that they can be reconstructed. The figures in parentheses refer to the Ludwig motet numbers. The contents are arranged in the following manner:

I. ....

Creatoris gratia	(540d)	(f. 1^r 1-6)
T. (Agmina)		(f. 1^r 6-8)

---

[1] L. A. Dittmer, *The Worcester Fragments*, 1957, Nr. 93. Ich möchte der Kapitelsbibliothek in Worcester, der Bodleian Library in Oxford, dem British Museum in London und der Universitätsbibliothek der University of Chicago meinen herzlichsten Dank für ihre Beihilfen in der Verwirklichung des vorliegenden Bandes aussprechen.

[1] L. A. Dittmer, *The Worcester Fragments*, 1957, No. 93. I should like to express my extreme thanks to the Chapter Library in Worcester, the Bodleian Library in Oxford, the British Museum in London and to the Library of the University of Chicago, which aided me enormously in the realisation of this volume.

Gegebenenfalls kann der zweite Teil des Motetus mit der verlorenen Komposition identisch sein, deren Textanfang *O Maria vas munditie* in dem Register in British Museum, *Harley 978* [1]) verzeichnet ist.

The second part of this motetus could be identical with the lost composition, the incipit of whose text *O Maria vas munditie* is to be found in the index in British Museum, *Harley 978* [1]).

II. ....
Dona celi factor (358a) (f. 1^r 8-10)
T.............. (.....f. 1^r 11)

Der Text des Motetus dieser Komposition ist anderweitig in den Westminster Fragmenten *33327* bekannt [2]); gegebenenfalls kann der verlorene Triplumtext dieser Komposition mit jener identisch sein. Wir haben hier wiederum ein Beispiel, wie Worcester Nr. 40 und 70, wo die Motettentexte einer zu einem Choralabschnitt gesetzten Motette wieder komponiert werden, ohne dass der letztere Gesang mit einer Choralmelodie verbunden ist; man möchte in diesen Fällen glauben, dass der mit einer Choralmelodie versehene Gesang französischen Ursprungs, der andere englischer Herkunft ist.

The text of the motetus of this composition is otherwise known in the Westminster Fragments *33327* [2]); perhaps the missing text of the triplum of this composition may be identical with that one. Again, we have an example, like Worcester Nos. 40 and 70, where the texts set to one of the motets (where the tenor is based on a gregorian section) have been recomposed, whereby the latter version has no connection with any gregorian melody; one would like to believe, that the composition with a liturgical sequence of pitches is French in origin, the other English.

III. In excelsis gloria (f. 1^v 1-5)
In excelsis gloria (f. 1^v 6-11)
In excelsis gloria (f. 2^r 1-4)

Diesen Rondellus, dessen Text nicht mit dem gleichbeginnenden *Chevalier 8585* identisch ist, trifft man wieder als Worcester Nr. 93, wo er übertragen wird.

One finds this rondellus, the text of which is not identical with the one beginning similarly *Chevalier 8585*, again as Worcester No. 93, where it is transcribed.

---

1) Vgl. L. A. Dittmer, ***An English Discantuum Volumen,*** in Musica Disciplina, VIII 1954, S. 42.

2) Vgl. Band V dieser Reihe (***Worcester Add. 68 Westminster Abbey 33327*** und ***Madrid, Bibl. nac. 192)*** S. 83-86.

1) Cf. L. A. Dittmer, ***An English Discantuum Volumen,*** in Musica Disciplina, VIII 1954, p. 42.

2) Cf. Volume V of this series (***Worcester Add. 68, Westminster Abbey 33327*** and ***Madrid, Bibl. nac. 192***) p. 83-86.

IV. Spiritus et alme (f. 2^r 5-7)
Gaude virgo salutata (f. 2^r 8-10)
Tenor (f. 2^r 10-12)

Dem Gloriatropus *Spiritus et alme,* der in verschiedenen mehrstimmigen Kompositionen um diese Zeit in England vorzufinden ist [1], begegnet man als *Chevalier 19312,* dazu auch *Chevalier* Band VI S. 373, zum ersten Male hier als Motettentext. Der Motetus ist *Chevalier 7029,* dazu auch Band VI S. 168 und ist anderweitig als eine isolierte Motettenstimme in Oxford, *Bodleian Library, Corpus Christi College 497* f. 6^v in einer musikalisch abweichenden Fassung zu finden. Der Tenor, der wohl einen *cantus prius factus* enthalten kann, konnte vorläufig nicht identifiziert werden.

The trope to the gloria *Spiritus et alme,* which is found in quite a few polyphonic compositions in England at this time [1], is found as *Chevalier 19312,* compare also *Chevalier* Vol. VI p. 373, and is used here for the first time for a motet-text. The motetus is *Chev. 7029,* compare also Vol. VI p. 168 and is otherwise known as an isolated motet-voice in Oxford, *Bodleian Library, Corpus Christi College 497* f. 6^v in a different musical setting. The tenor, which could contain a *cantus prius factus,* could not be identified for the time being.

V. Stella maris (f. 2^v 1-4)
Stella maris (f. 2^v 5-7)
Stella maris (f. 2^v 8-12)

Rondellus; eine der frühesten Kompositionen mit unabhängigen Einsätzen der einzelnen Stimmen.

Rondellus; one of the earliest examples of compositions with independent entries of the individual voices.

VI. Patris superni gratia (f. 3^r 1-4)
Patris superni gratia (f. 3^r 5-8)
Pia pacis inclita (f. 3^r 9-11)

VII. Orbis pium primordium (f. 3^v 1-6)
Orbis pium primordium (f. 3^v 6-11)
Ovi patitum pretum (f. 4^r 1-4)

VIII. Barbara simplex animo (f. 4^r 5-7)
Barbara simplex animo (f. 4^r 8-10)
Tenor (f. 4^r 11-12)

---

1) Vgl. L. A. Dittmer, in *Musica Disciplina,* VIII 1954, S. 39.

1) Cf. L. A. Dittmer, in *Musica Disciplina,* VIII 1954, p. 39.

IX. Christi cara mater (f. 4^{v} 1-6)
Christi cara mater (f. 4^{v} 7-11)
(Christi cara mater)

Im Gegensatz zu den kontinentalen Kompositionen der damaligen Zeit findet man in diesen Gesängen grössere Melismen wie im Notre-Dame Conductus, den Rondellussatz mit seinem Stimmtausch, dem freierfundenen Tenor neben dem liturgischen sowie die eigentlichen Motettenkompositionen. Soweit ersichtlich, entbehrt dieses Repertoire die streng liturgischen Kompositionen, Choralbearbeitungen des *proprium* wie *ordinarium missae,* wie wir sie in den Worcester Fragmenten finden; doch bleiben die Kompositionen konservativ und geistlich; nicht weniger als fünf Texte beziehen sich auf die heilige Jungfrau. Durch diese Fragmente werden die Quellen der insularen Mehrstimmigkeit um die Wende zum 14. Jahrhundert um eine vermehrt und der englische Beitrag zur mittelalterlichen Musikgeschichte weiter geklärt.

In contradistinction to the continental compositions of the period in question, one finds larger melismata in these settings as also in the Notre-Dame conductus, furthermore the compositional technique of the rondellus, the freely composed tenor as well as the liturgical one, in addition to these, actual motet-settings. As far as can be seen, this répertoire avoids the strictly liturgical compositions, *organa* of the *proprium* and *ordinarium missae,* as we find among the Worcester Fragments; nevertheless, these compositions remain conservative and religious; no fewer than five texts are dedicated to the Holy Virgin. By virtue of these fragments, the sources of insular polyphony around the turn to the 14th century have been increased and the English contribution to mediaeval musical history further elucidated.

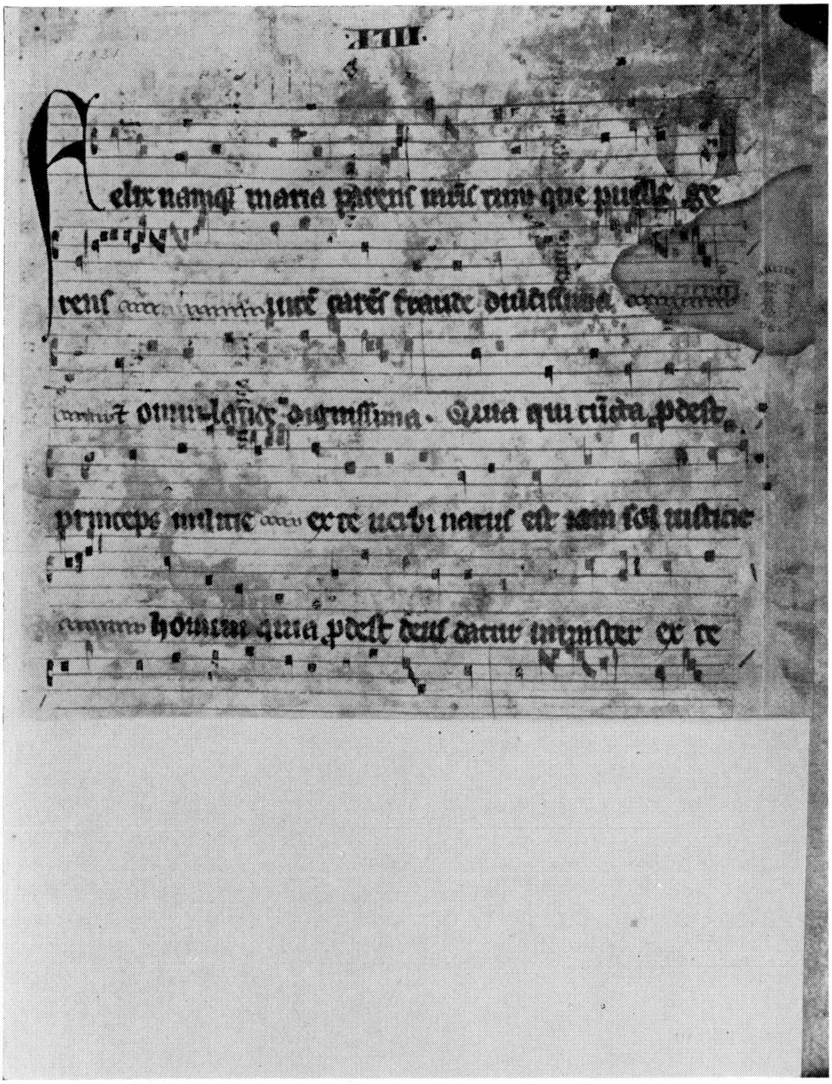

London, British Museum, Add. 25031 f. 2c^{v} (3^{r})

a

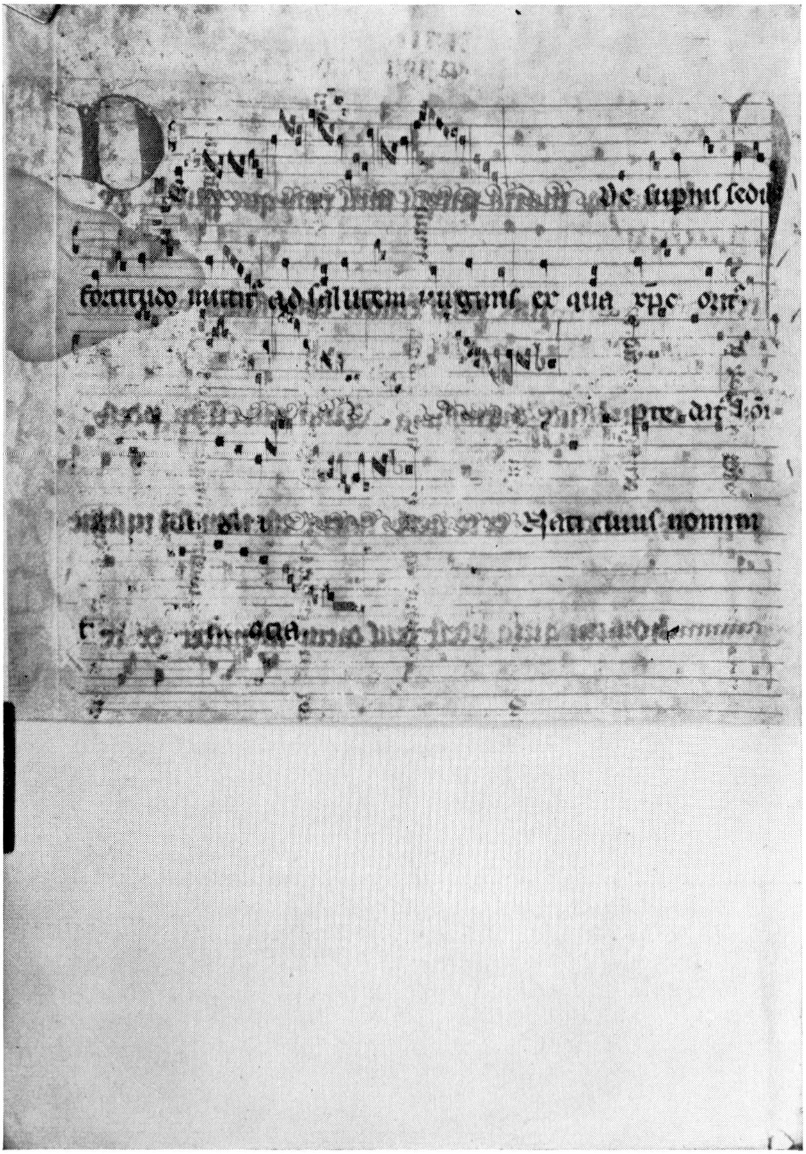

London, British Museum, Add. 25031 f. 2c^r (3^v)

b

London, British Museum, Add. 25031 f. 3^{r} (4^{v})

c

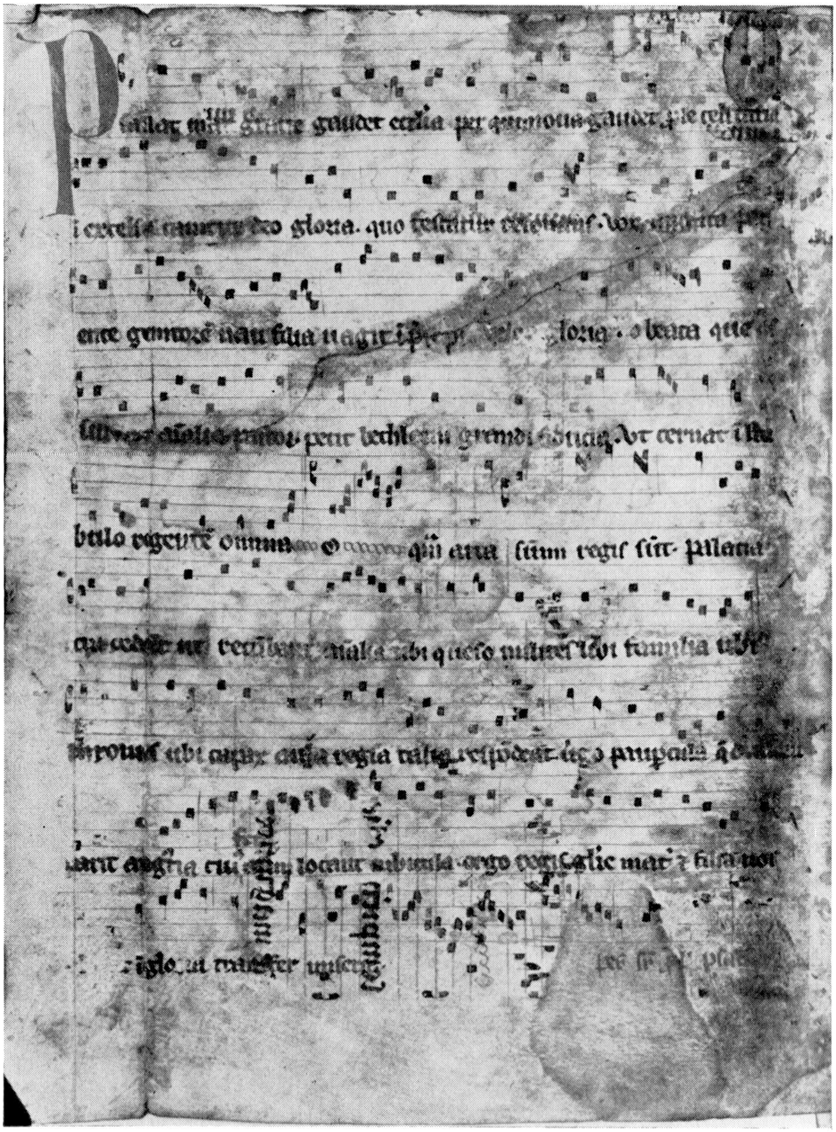

London, British Museum, Add. 25031 f. 1r (5r)

d

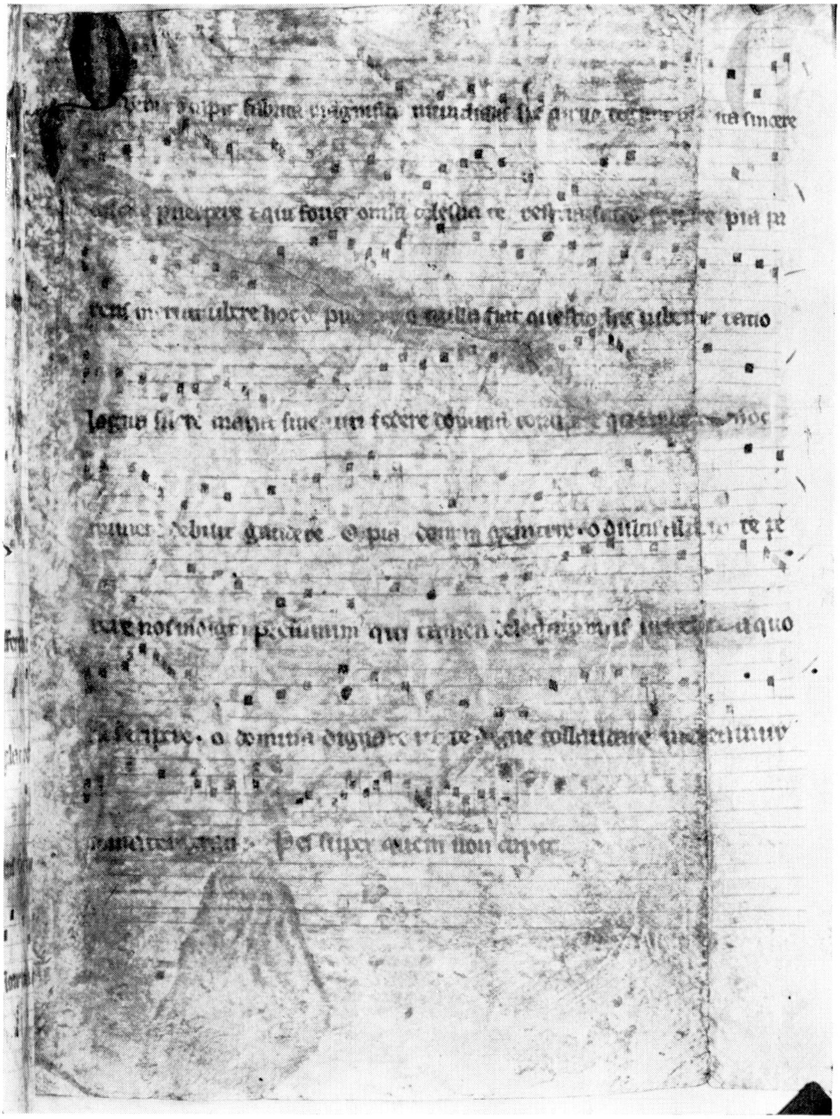

London, British Museum, Add. 25031 f. 1v (5v)

e

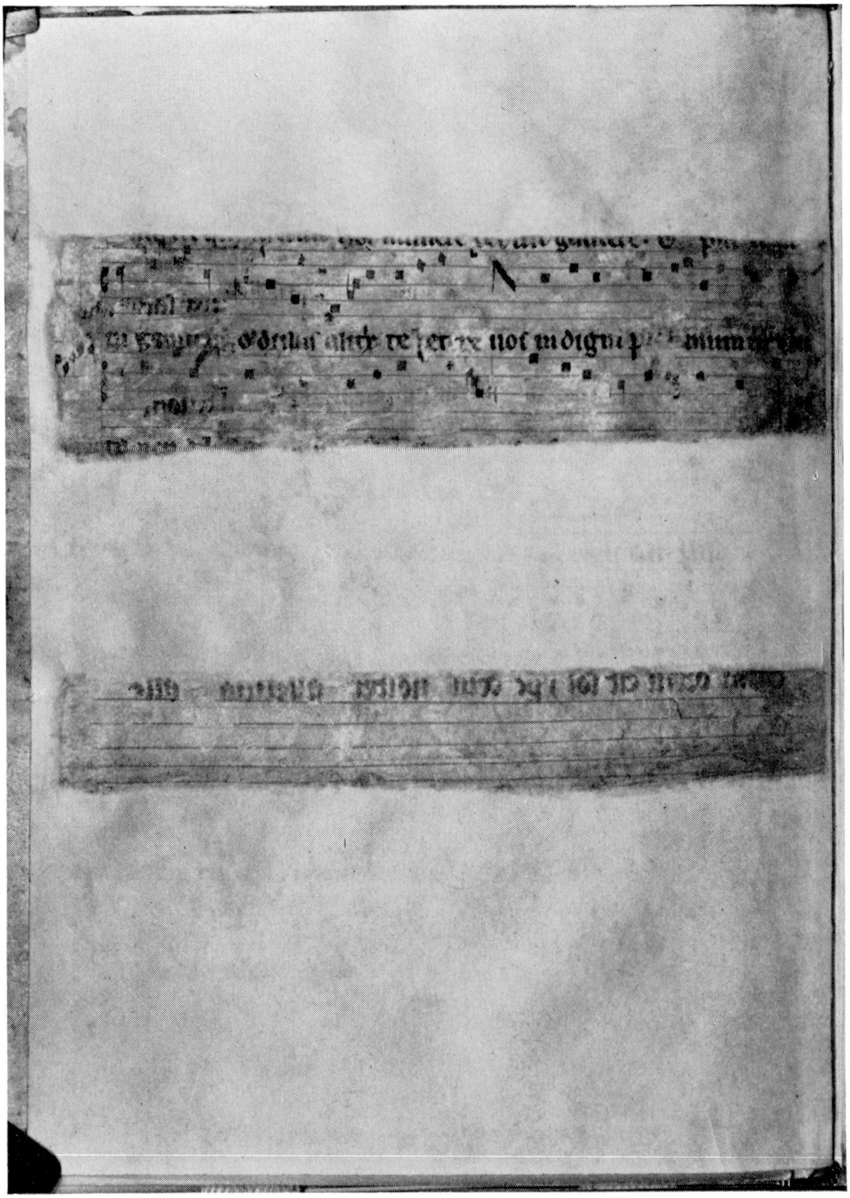

London, British Museum, Add. 25031 f. 2a^{r} & 2b^{v} (6^{r})

f

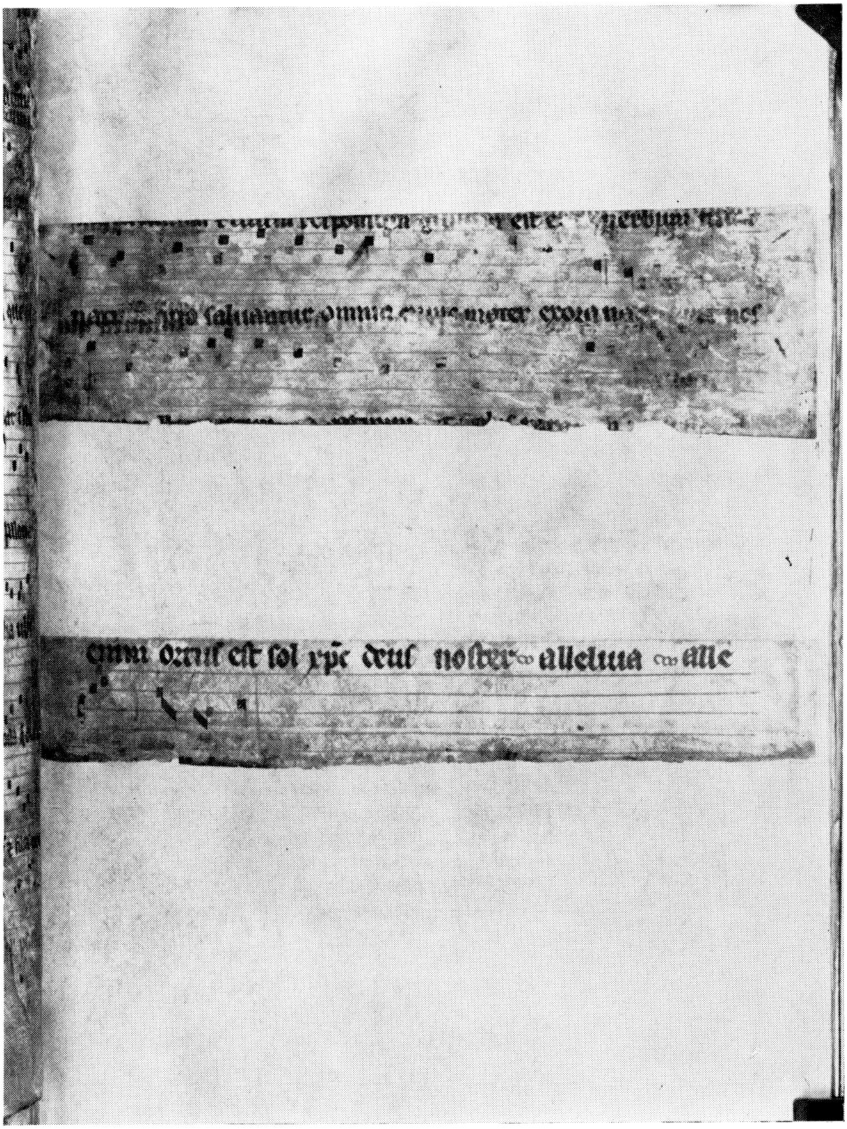

London, British Museum, Add. 25031 f. 2a[v] & 2a[r] (6[v])

g

Worcester, Chapter Library, Add. 68 Fragment XXVIII f. 1a[v] (8[v])

h

Oxford, Bodleian Library, Latin Liturgical d 20 f. 12^{r}

i

Oxford, Bodleian Library, Latin Liturgical d 20 f. 12v

k

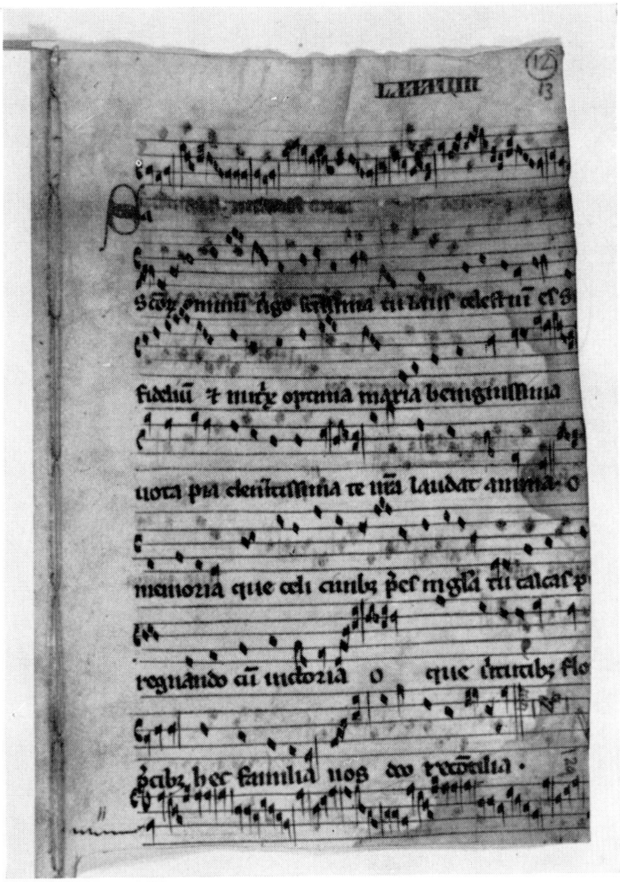

Oxford, Bodleian Library, Latin Liturgical d 20 f. 13^r

1

Oxford, Bodleian Library, Latin Liturgical d 20 f. 13v

m

Oxford, Bodleian Library, Latin Liturgical d 20 f. 14r

n

Oxford, Bodleian Library, Latin Liturgical d 20 f. 14v

O

Oxford, Bodleian Library, Latin Liturgical d 20 f. 15r

p

Oxford, Bodleian Library, Latin Liturgical d 20 f. 15v

9

Oxford, Bodleian Library, Latin Liturgical d 20 f. 16r

r

Oxford, Bodleian Library, Latin Liturgical d 20 f. 17r

s

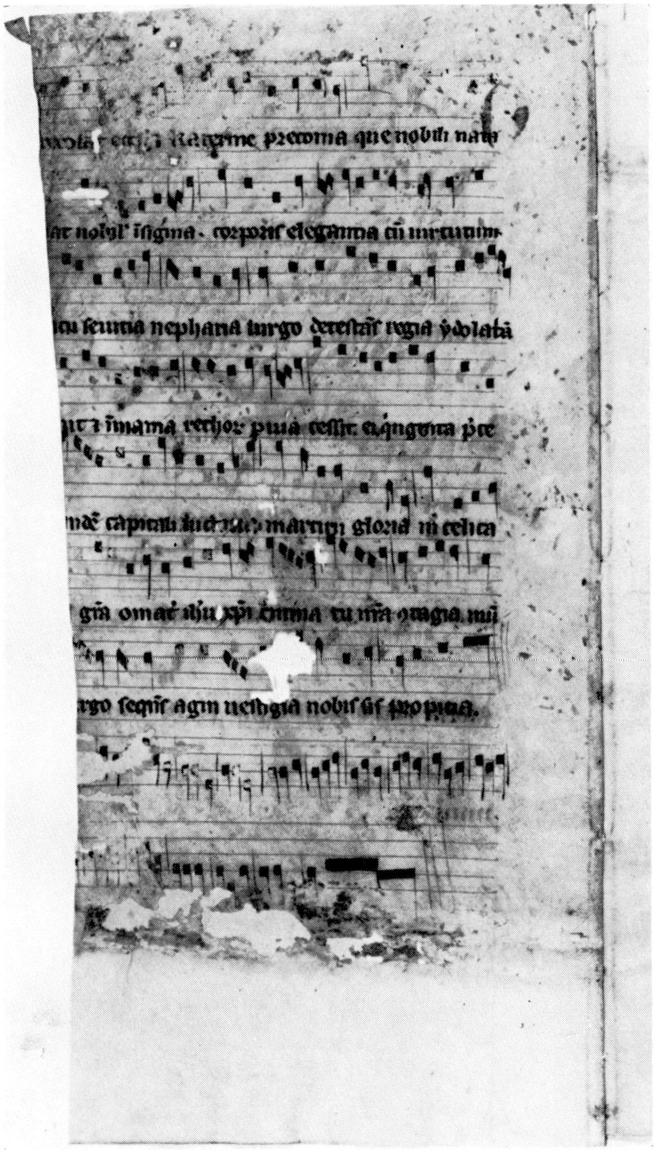

Oxford, Bodleian Library, Latin Liturgical d 20 f. 18v

t

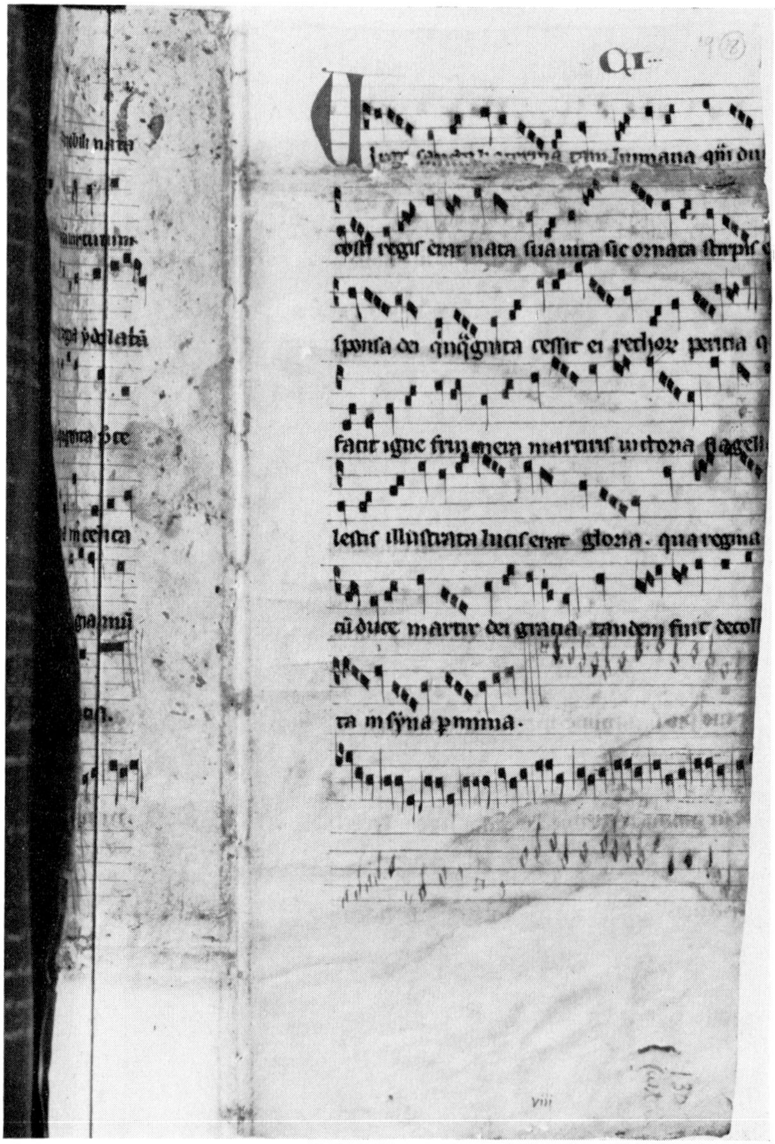

Oxford, Bodleian Library, Latin Liturgical d 20 f. 19^{r}

u

Oxford, Bodleian Library, Latin Liturgical d 20 f. 19v

V

Worcester, Chapter Library, Add. 68 Fragment XI f. 2^{r} (21^{r})

W

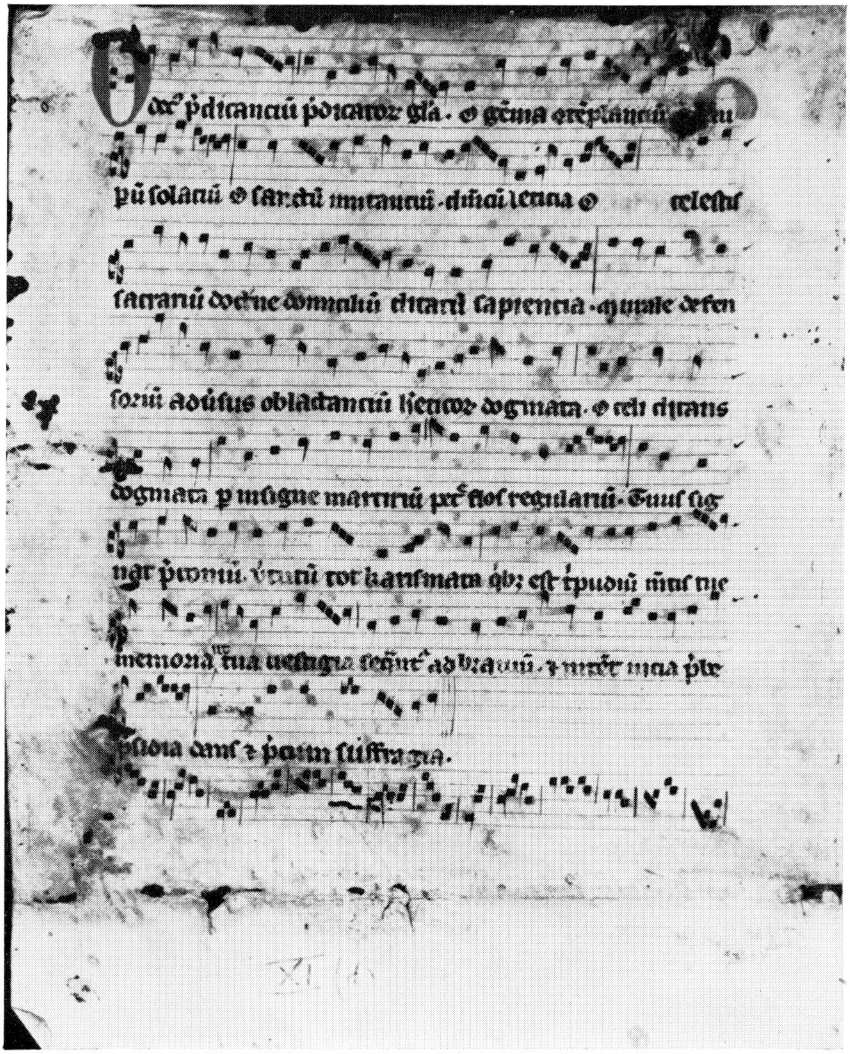

Worcester, Chapter Library, Add. 68 Fragment XI f. 2v (21v)

x

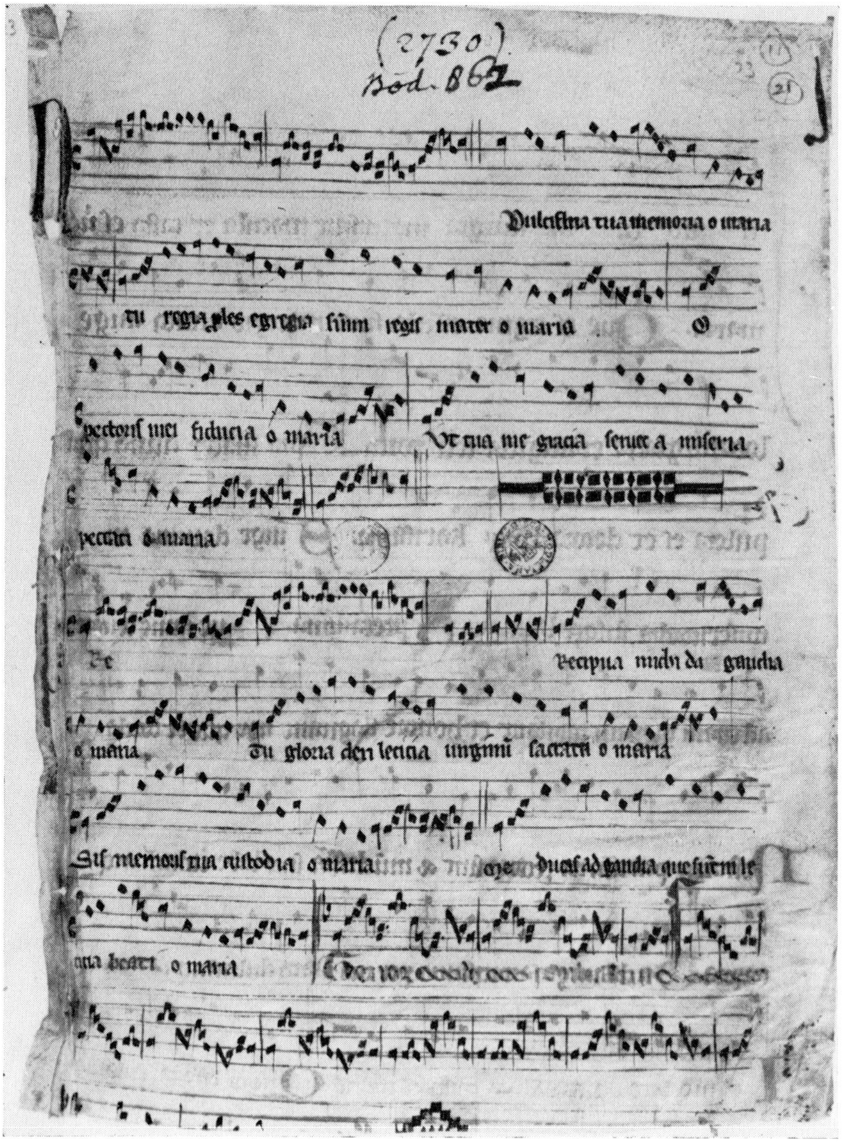

Oxford, Bodleian Library, Latin Liturgical d 20 f. 23r

y

Oxford, Bodleian Library, Latin Liturgical d 20 f. 23^{v}

z

Oxford, Bodleian Library, Latin Liturgical d 20 f. 24r

aa

Oxford, Bodleian Library, Latin Liturgical d 20 f. 24v

bb

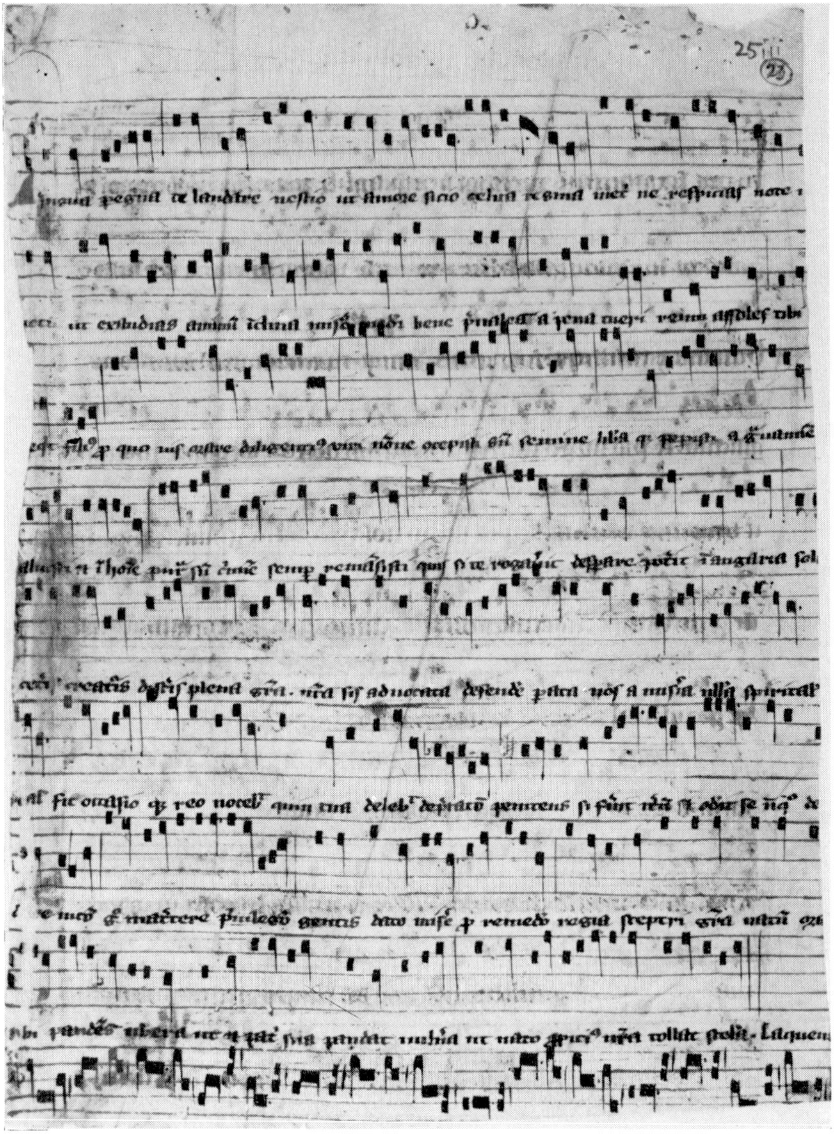

Oxford, Bodleian Library, Latin Liturgical d 20 f. 25r

cc

Oxford, Bodleian Library, Bodley 862 hinterer Deckel seitenverkehrt (27a^{v})
rear cover reversed

ee

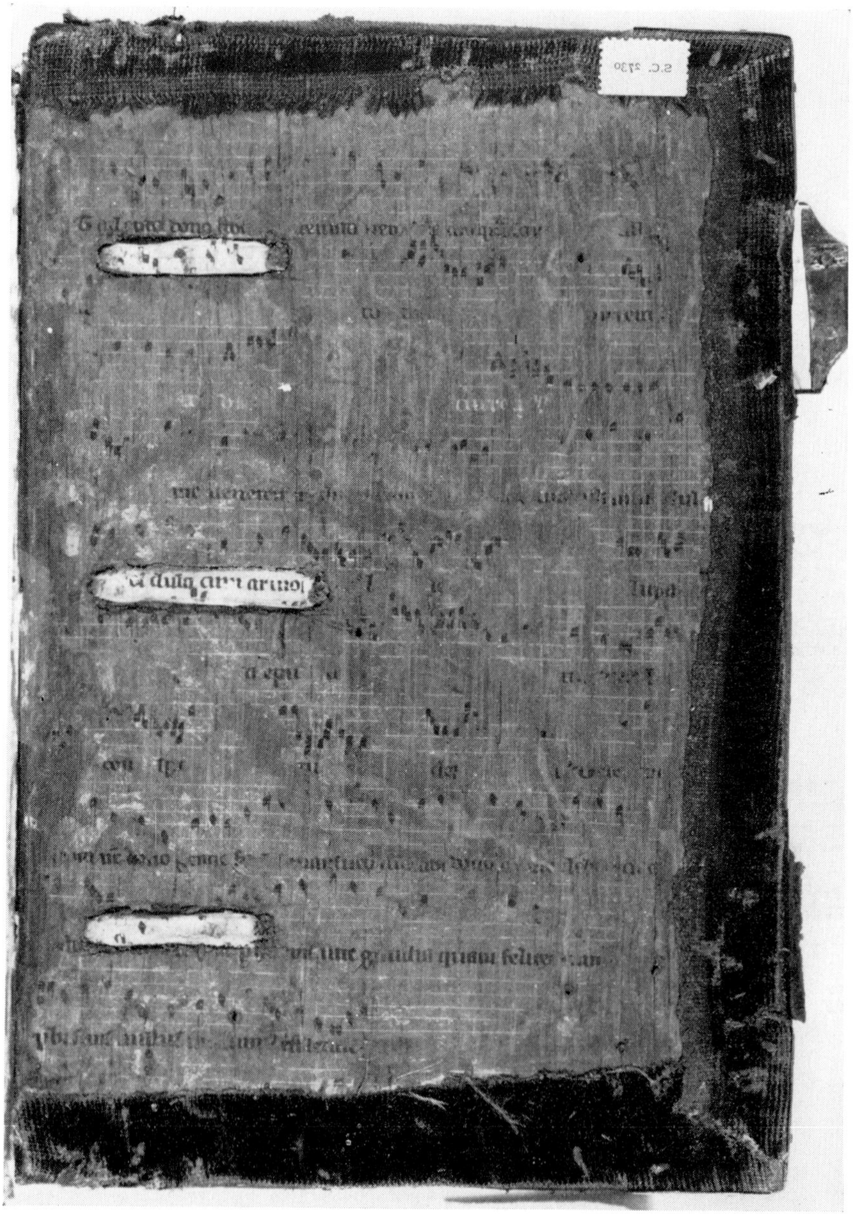

Oxford, Bodleian Library, Bodley 862 vorderer Deckel seitenverkehrt (27a^r)
front cover reversed

dd

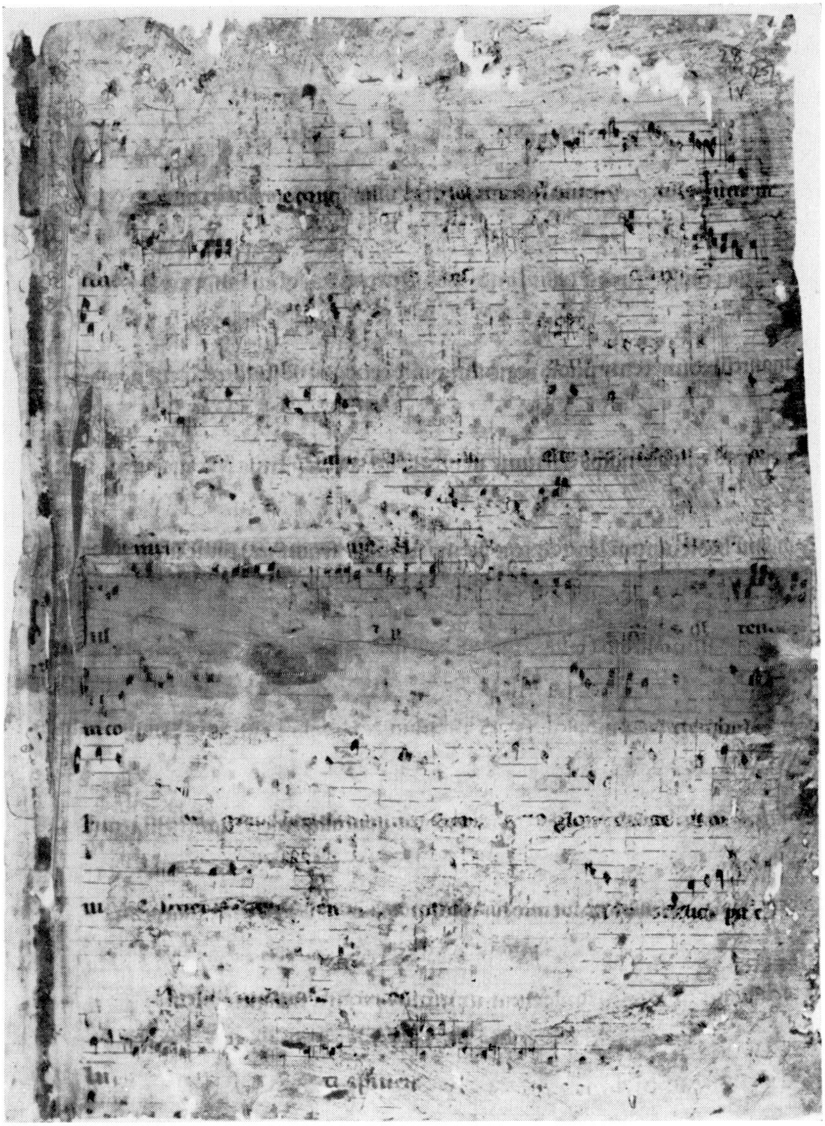

Oxford, Bodleian Library, Latin Liturgical d 20 f. 28r

ff

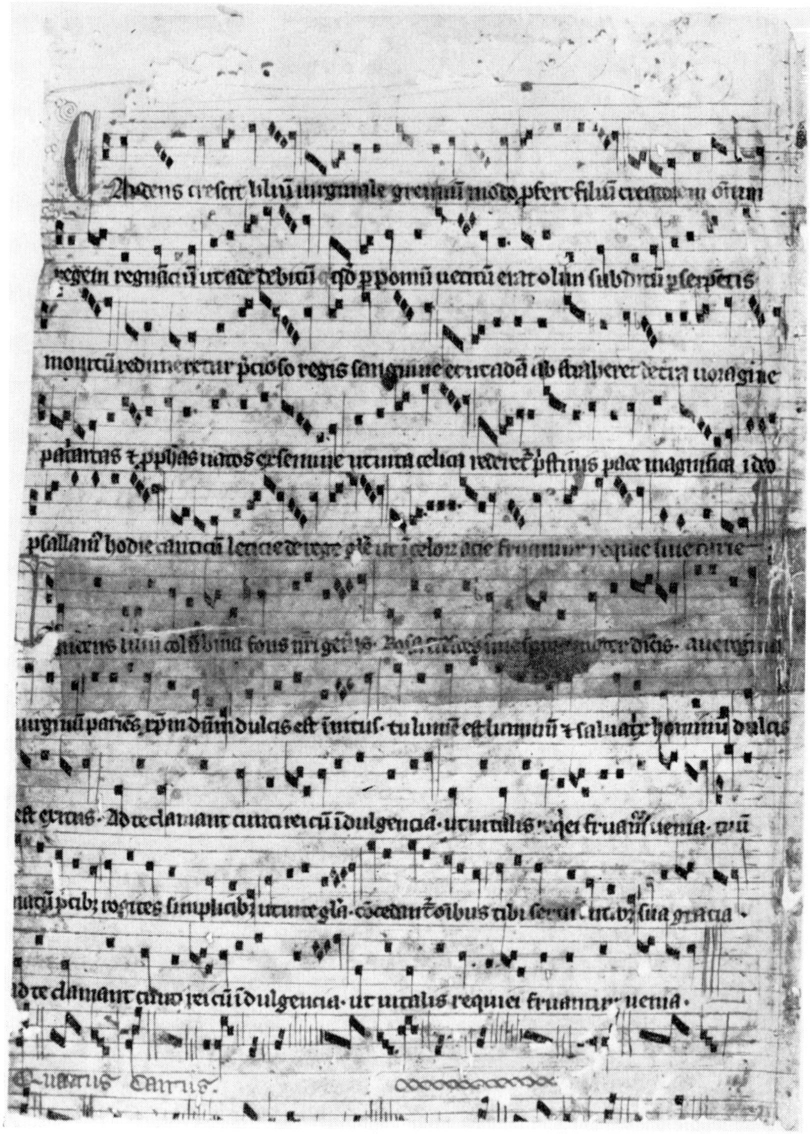

Oxford, Bodleian Library, Latin Liturgical d 20 f. 28v

gg

Oxford, Bodleian Library, Latin Liturgical d 20 ff. 34r & 34v

ii & kk

Oxford, Bodleian Library, Latin Liturgical d 20 f. 35r

II

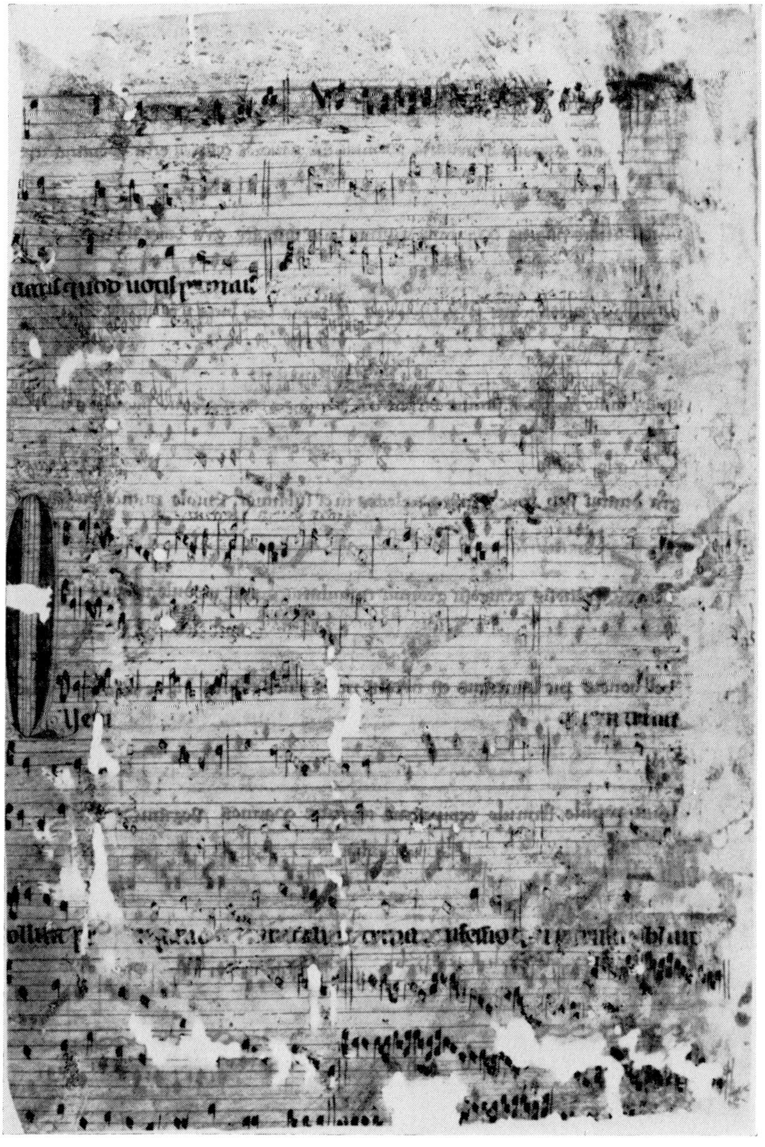

Oxford, Bodleian Library, Latin Liturgical d 20 f. 35v

mm

Worcester, Chapter Library, Add. 68 Fragment XXXII recto

nn

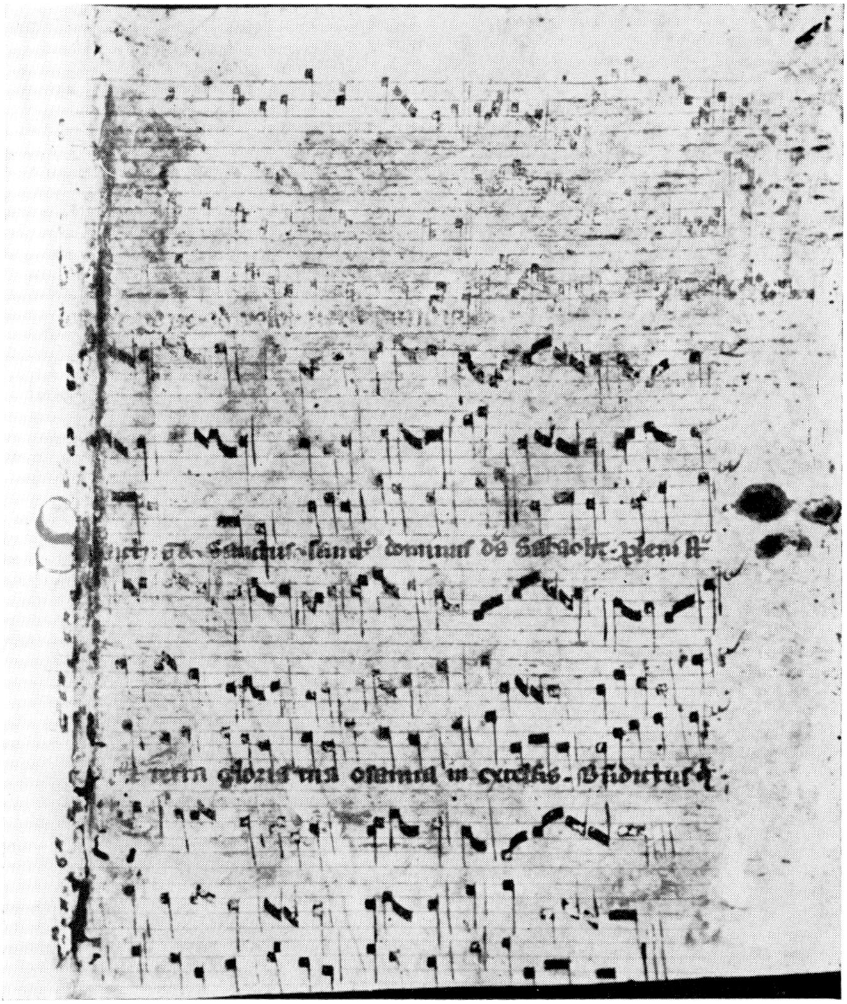

Worcester, Chapter Library, Add. 68 Fragment XXXII verso

oo

Chicago, University of Chicago Library, Ms. 654app f. 1r

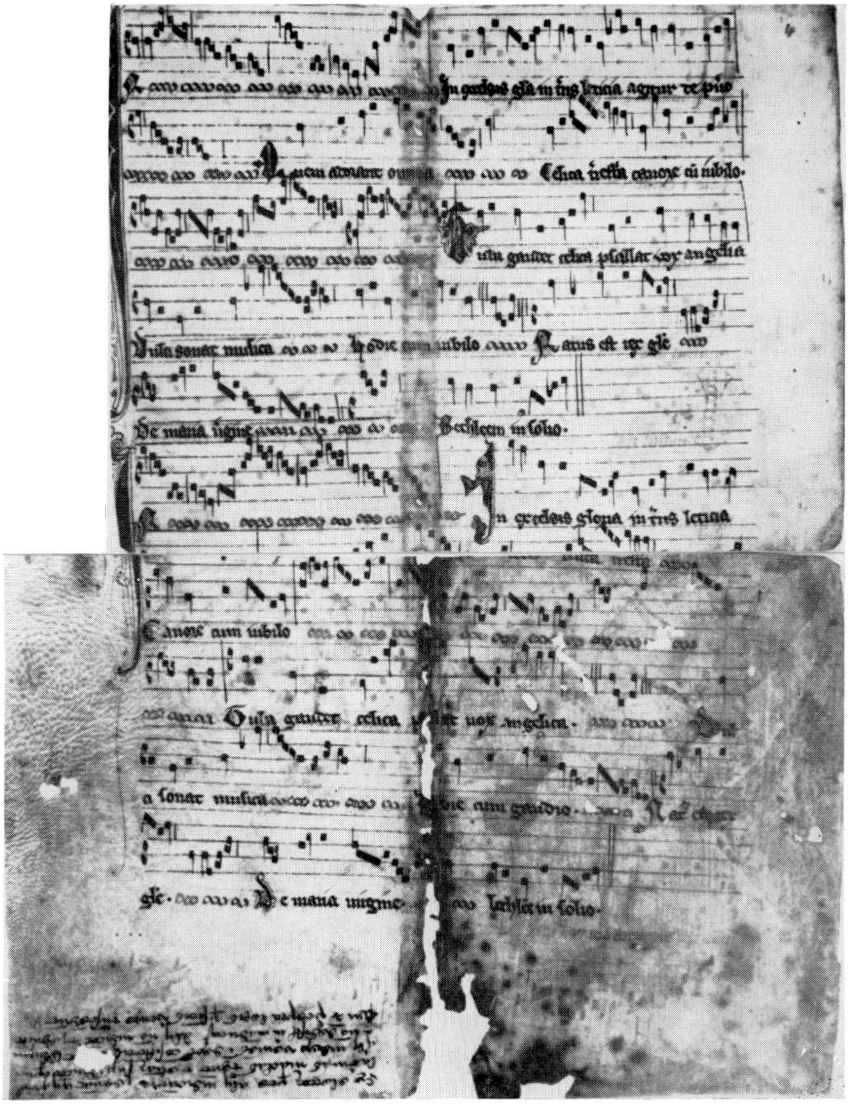

Chicago, University of Chicago Library, Ms. 654app. f. 1^{v}

Chicago, University of Chicago Library, Ms. 654app. f. 2r

Chicago, University of Chicago Library, Ms. 654app. f 2v

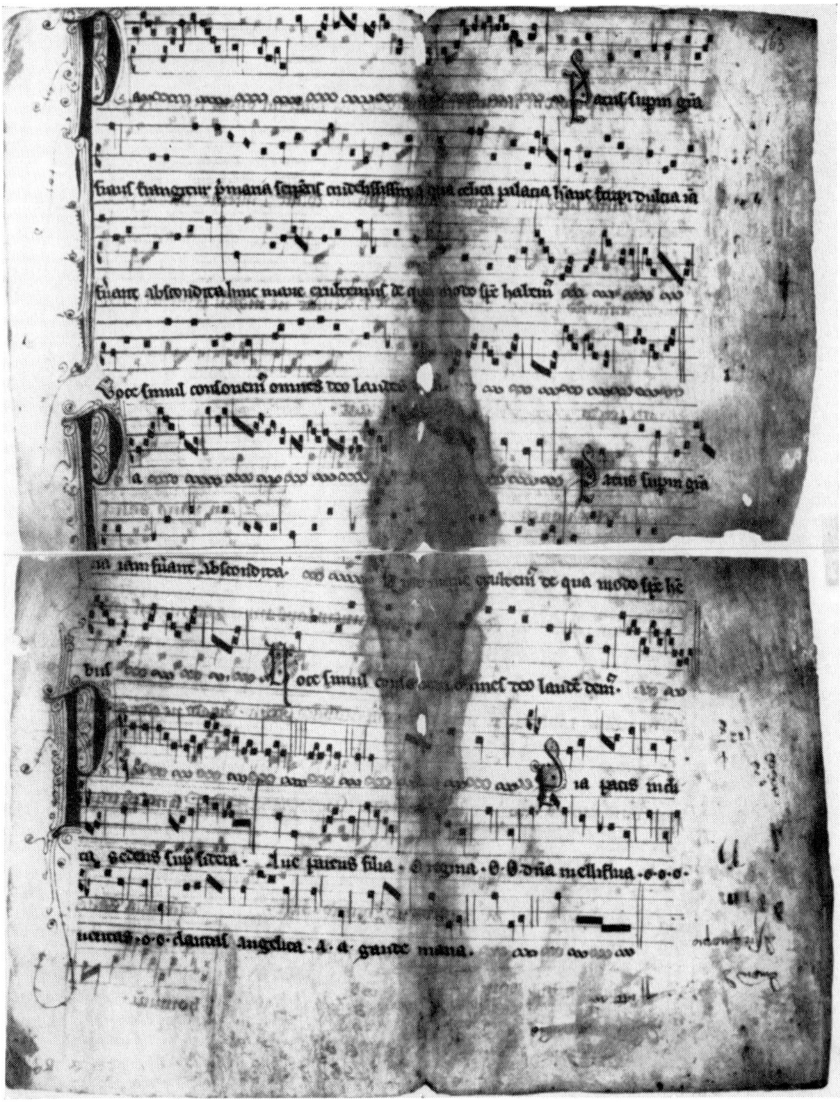

Chicago, University of Chicago Library, Ms. 654app. f. 3r

Chicago, University of Chicago Library, Ms. 654app. f 3v

Chicago, University of Chicago Library, Ms. 654app. f. 4r

Chicago, University of Chicago Library, Ms. 654app. f. 4v

Creatoris gratia .... (Agmina)

Nobis aperi Venam veni - e Vena pe-ni-ten-ti - e, Per quam
in-gre-di que - a-mus vi-te ca - cu - mi - na, Abs - que di -
u cru-ci - a-tis verberami - na Iam suscipe pi - a lau - dem
car - mi - na. O Ma - ri-a, Vas mun-di-ci - e, Ro - re fe -
cun-di - da mi-se - re-ri - e, Et gra-ti - e, Lis ad - iutrix,
Pre-ce pi - a Tu fi-de - li fa - mi - li - e, Quam se-cu-ras die

Dona celi (-ie ineffabilis) (Tenor)

Spiritus et alme   Gaude virgo   Tenor

Tenor

10
8 pa - ra-cli - te, Pri - mo - ge - ni tus
8 nun - ci - o, Gau - de ma - ter
8
15
Ma - ri - e vir - gi - nis ma -
jo - cun-da - ta Ie - sum pu - er-pe - ri -
20
tris, Ad Ma - ri - e glo - ri - am
o Gau - de conresu-ci - ta - ta Re - sur -
25
Ma - ri - am san -
gen-te fi-li - o. Gaude tu- a sub-li-ma-ta pro - le

30
cti - fi - cans, Ma - ri - - - am gu -
plena gau-di - o Gau-de sumpta et lo - cata Cum Ie-
35
ber - nans, Ma - ri - am
sum in so - li - o, E-sto no-bis ad - vo - cata
40
In ma - gno iu - di-ci - o
45
co - ro - nans.

5
S
tella maris nuncupa - ris
S
tella maris
S
10
15
nuncupa - ris
Tu que cel-se
tella maris nuncupa - ris
20
25
coro-na - ris
Tu que cel-se coro-na - ris
Tu que celse coro-na -
30
Va-le vir - go glo - ri - e.
O quam sa-crum pignus
Vale vir - go glo-ri - e.
ris Va-le virgo glo - ri - e.

35
pa - ris
O quam sa-crum pignus pa - ris
O quam sacrum pignus pa -
40
45
Portus summi salu - ta - ris
Portus sum-mi sa-lu-ta - ris
ris
Portus summi saluta -
Que cum nato salu-ta - ris
Que cum nato gratu - la - ris
ris
Que cum na - to gratula-
55
Partus tui pu-el-la - ris Ob virtutem in-pre-la - ris
Partus tu-i
ris

60
puellaris Per virtutem inpre-la - ris
Partus tui pu-el-la -
65
Transfer tuos ho - di - e.
Transfer tuos ho - di - e.
ris Per virtu-tem impre - la - ris Ho - di - e.
Patris superni Patris superni Pia pacis
5
Pa -
Pa -
Pi -
10

15
20
Pa -tris super - ni grati-a Fraus
Pa - tris super-ni grati-a Fraus frangi-
Pi - a pa - cis in-cli -
25
frangitur pri ma-ri-a Serpentis crude - lis-si-ma Qua ce-li-ca pa -
tur pri maria Serpentis cru-de - lis - sima Qua celi-ca
ta Sedens su -pra si - de -
30
35
la-ti - a stirpi dulci-a Iam fu-e -rant abscondi-
pa-la - ti-a stirpi dulci-a Iam fu-e - rant abscondi-
ra Ave pa - rens fi - li -

40
ta. Hinc Ma-ri - e exul - temus, De qua modo spem ha-be-mus,
ta.
a. O re - gi - na, O O
45
Hinc Mari-e exul - temus, De qua modo spem habe - mus
do - mi - na mel - li-flu-a, O O
50
Vo-ce si - mul consone-mus O - mnes deo lau-des demus.
O ve-ri - tas, O O clari-tas an-ge-li-
55
Vo-ce si - mul consone - mus O - mnes deo laudes de - mus.
ca, a a Gau - de Ma - ri -

Orbis pium (Orbis pium) Ovi paritum

lat Et in - fe - rat Vi - tam ple-bi, Quam ti-tu - ban - do per-de -
in - fe-rat Vi - tam ple-bi, quam ti - tu - ban - do per-de -
mu - tam gen - tem, quam fe- ce -
rat. Dic an - te ne e - dat Sic de - si - nat; Ne mor-su pestife-
rat. Dic an - te ne e - dat Sic de - si - nat; Ne mor-su pe-stifero
rat, Et se- rum du-cit ut
Pre a - de-pta vi - ta pe - re - at. Ni - si
Pre a - de-pta vi - ta pe - re - at. Ni -
gau- de - at; Ni -
nos pa - ter re - spi - ci - at
si

50
nos pa - ter re - spi - ci - at
si
55
Di - cat plebs non
nos pa - ter re - spi - ci - at
60
est qui ad - u - ru - at
Di - cat plebs non est qui ad - u -
65
70
Nam va - na sa -
ru-at
Nam vana sa-
Di-cat plebs non est qui ad - u - ru - at
Nam va-

Barbara simplex animo **Barbara simplex animo** **Tenor**

Do - mi-ni.
Do - mi-ni.
O - mnes sa-crate virginis Fe-dentes sponso lampades
O - mnes sa-crate virginis Fe - dentes sponso lampades
Vasis te - nen-tes o - le - um
Vasis te - nen-tes o - le - um
Me - um que - ra-tis con - mo - dum.
Me - um que - ra - tis con - mo - dum.

Christi cara mater
Christi cara mater
(Christi cara mater)
Chri -
Chri -
Chri -

Christi cara mater a - ve Ma-ri -
a mun - dis-si- ma
Christi cara mater a - ve Ma-ri - a mun -
dis-si - ma
Christi cara mater a - ve Ma-ri - a mun - dis-si -
Que tam sacrum tam suave pondus profers inte- gra
Tutu- o - rum nunc servorum
ma

Can -
Can -

Cantu novo nunc in choro concrepemus panitur
Cantu novo nunc in choro
concrepemus panitur
Cantu novo nunc in choro concrepemus pani-tur
Notas me . . . .
Et Ma-ri-e matri pi-e
iubi-lemus iugitur.
. . . .

UNSERE VERÖFFENTLICHUNGEN OUR PUBLICATIONS

VERÖFFENTLICHUNGEN MITTELALTERLICHER MUSIKHANDSCHRIFTEN

PUBLICATIONS OF MEDIAEVAL MUSICAL MANUSCRIPTS

Vol. I	Madrid 20486	$ 8.00
Vol. II	Wolfenbüttel 1099	$ 40.00
Vol. III	Eine zentrale Quelle der Notre-Dame Musik A Central Source of Notre-Dame Polyphony	$ 15.00
Vol. IV	Paris, nouv. acq. fr. 13521 & lat. 11411	$ 7.50
Vol. V	Worcester Add. 68, Westminster 33327 & Madrid 192	$ 9.00
Vol. VI	Oxford, lat. lit. d 20 & Chicago, 654app	$ 12.00
Vol. VII	Opera omnia Faugues	$ 15.00

MUSICAL THEORISTS IN TRANSLATION

Vol. I	Anonymous IV	$ 7.50
Vol. II	Robert de Handlo	$ 7.00
Vol. III	Johannes de Garlandia	$ 7.50
Vol. IV	Marchettus de Padua, *Pomerium*	$ 7.50

GESAMTAUSGABEN — COLLECTED WORKS

Vol. I	Faugues (Gesamtausgabe, Collected Works)	$ 15.00

WISSENSCHAFTLICHE ABHANDLUNGEN MUSICOLOGICAL STUDIES

Vol. I	L. Dittmer, *Auszug aus The Worcester Music Fragments*	$ 1.00
Vol. II	G. Schuetze, *An Introduction to Faugues*	$ 10.50
Vol. III	E. Trumble, *Fauxbourdon, an Historical Survey*, I	$ 7.50

MIKROFILME — MICROFILMS

I	Studies of Music in the Middle Ages (Gennrich, Wagner)	$ 18.00
II	U. Chevalier, *Repertorium hymnologicum*, I-VI	$ 12.00

Printed in the Netherlands by Royal VanGorcum Ltd., Assen
from clichées prepared by the Institute of Mediaeval Music, New York, U.S.A.